Generational Planning

Creating and Perpetuating Wealth For Generations

Brian Skrobonja

Generational Planning

Printed by:
CreateSpace Independent
Publishing Platform

Published in the United States of America

Book ID: 160829-00523

ISBN-13:978-1542910675
ISBN-10:1542910676

Here's What's Inside...

Introduction 1

What Would the Rockefellers Do? 3

Why Aren't More Families Able To
Create Wealth For Generations? 7

Generational Planning..9

The Danger in Waiting
to Figure Everything Out 12

Generational Planning Mindset 15

Keeping the Money Together............................26

Myths and Mistakes Surrounding
Generational Planning 31

How to Create and Perpetuate
Wealth For Generations... 37

Improve Your Mindset 39

About the Author - Brian Skrobonja...............40

Introduction

Generational Planning

When it comes to generational planning, what I have found is that many people desire to leave their kids and grandkids better positioned financially, spiritually, and with wisdom to make their lives better than their own.

However, it is most often wishful thinking, since many people spend very little time thinking about their legacy, taking action to transfer assets, instill their values and their wisdom to the next generation.

I have found that people often live as if money, their beliefs, their values, and their wishes are secret and seldom do much of anything to organize and communicate them to their children or grandchildren.

An unfortunate roadblock to the entire idea of generational planning is that many people will miss the opportunity to enhance the next generation by living with a scarcity mindset and a lack of confidence to lead their family.

For us to leave a legacy and enhance the next generation, we must begin to realize that living in scarcity and keeping our wishes for future generations a secret leaves the next generation starting over; the pattern of scarcity and secrecy is repeated generation after generation.

My hope is by reading this book, your mindset for what is possible will be expanded and you will allow yourself to think beyond simply distributing what you have to your kids or favorite charity at your death. When you think in terms of generations, you not only impact the next generation but all future generations.

To Your Success!

What Would the Rockefellers Do?

In Garrett Gunderson and Michael Isom's book titled, *What Would the Rockefellers Do?*, the authors shared the story of two families, the Vanderbilts and the Rockefellers.

Cornelius Vanderbilt made his fortune in the transportation business, starting by ferrying goods and passengers around New York Harbor in the early 19th century. Soon his business expanded to shipping goods from the West Coast to the East Coast, using Nicaragua as a passageway. Eventually, he switched from ships to trains, where he made his largest fortune yet in the railroad business. At his death in 1877, Vanderbilt's fortune was estimated to top $100 million, which was more than the US Treasury held at the time. That's more than $200 billion-with-a-"B" in today's dollars.

But even as the richest man in America, Vanderbilt lived a relatively modest life. He gave some money to charity—he donated $1 million to help start Vanderbilt University, and he also donated to churches. But 95% of his fortune was passed on to his son, William Henry Vanderbilt, leaving his surviving wife and children to split the rest.

William Henry Vanderbilt did well, doubling the family fortune before his death, nine years after the passing of his father. But that was the last time the Vanderbilt family fortune would grow. The Vanderbilt heirs became known as wealthy socialites with a penchant for lavish spending. There were ten Vanderbilt mansions built in Manhattan, including the largest private residence ever built there, plus several more around the country. Many of these homes seemed more like palaces, such as The Breakers in Newport, Rhode Island, which still stands today. But without any new money coming in, the fortune couldn't survive the spendthrift Vanderbilt heirs. By 1947, all ten Vanderbilt Manhattan mansions had been torn down.

It is said that Cornelius Vanderbilt's last words were, "Keep the money together." But the Vanderbilt heirs failed fabulously. The family fortune was squandered in a handful of generations. A direct descendant of Cornelius died broke 48 years after he did.

John D. Rockefeller made his fortune selling oil and kerosene. He started Standard Oil of Ohio in 1870, and by the end of the decade his business was refining more than 90% of the oil in the United States. Rockefeller's objective was to deliver the best oil at the cheapest price. He once wrote to a partner, "We must ever remember we are refining oil for the poor man and he must have it cheap and good." And Rockefeller succeeded, pushing the price of oil down from 58 cents to eight cents a gallon.

The result was that Rockefeller became the richest man in American history. The New York Times said in Rockefeller's 1937 obituary that he had amassed more than $1.5 billion dollars. In today's dollars, estimates of his wealth vary between $243 billion and $341 billion. Rockefeller was a prolific giver, donating more than $530 million of his fortune to charity during his lifetime. He also left $460 million to his son, John D. Rockefeller Jr., otherwise known as "Junior," in 1917. Unlike the Vanderbilts, Junior kept the family money together by creating a trust for each of his children—a daughter and five sons. The bulk of the family fortune was put into these trusts, managed by a group of financial professionals referred to as the "Family Office", which would provide Junior's kids with interest income.

Six generations later, the "Family Office" is still managing the Rockefeller fortune, which is estimated to be more than $10 billion. More than 150 Rockefellers currently receive interest income from the family trusts. And the family is said to donate as much as $50 million per year to charity, carrying on the senior Rockefeller's tradition of philanthropy.

What made the difference? Why did the Rockefellers keep their fortune while the Vanderbilts lost everything? The answer, ironically, is that the Rockefellers heeded the last words of Vanderbilt. They did "keep the money together," using trusts as a legal tool to protect the fortune as much as possible from taxes, lawsuits and spendthrift heirs.

The lesson is clear. If you want to empower your children, grandchildren and great-grandchildren, don't simply leave them money to spend as they please. Keep the money together. Design trusts that direct how money can and cannot be spent. And pass on your values to the next generation so that your vision doesn't stop with you.

The two families show with crystal clarity the difference between traditional estate planning and generational planning and why "Keeping the money together" is so vitally important. Once the money is distributed, it is gone forever. By keeping the money together, you create an opportunity for future generations.

Why Aren't More Families Able To Create Wealth For Generations?

It has been my observation that the financial services industry has done a poor job with truly helping people with wealth transfer. The public, and many professional advisors, have limited thinking about how wealth is created and transferred upon death. The existing mindset around estate planning normally leads up to the death of one generation and then distributes the assets to the second generation, who is then free to use the assets in any way they choose.

In James Hughes' book, *Family Wealth*, Hughes describes a reoccurring pattern of families creating wealth in one generation, transferring it to the next generation who then consumes the wealth leaving nothing for the third and future generations. He calls it Rags to Rags in three generations.

The idea that someone creates wealth over a lifetime and, at their death, passes it to their kids without a plan for how the money is to be used is proof that more education is needed.

The problem, in my opinion, is the mindset that assumes everyone in the family knows what to do or a belief that things will be learned through osmosis. Under this mindset, there is no emphasis on educating family members about money, their beliefs, their values, or even the giver's wishes after they pass. Therefore, there is very little guidance given for what the receiving generation should do with the money coming their way.

All of this could very well be a result of not knowing that there is a way to plan generationally. So, it is my hope in writing this book that we can help families overcome the statistics by facilitating communication and developing strategies to create and perpetuate wealth for multiple generations.

Generational Planning

There is never a one-size-fits-all solution for how a generational plan is to be arranged. Family dynamics, their belief system, and their financial situation will dictate the details of a plan.

With that being said, the framework of a generational plan begins with the mindset of thinking beyond your death and accepting a broader vision for what is possible. It is abandoning the status quo of simply distributing assets at one's death and making a move toward the development of a strategy that has each generation both creating and perpetuating wealth for future generations.

It is a culture within each generation to accept the responsibility of educating and preparing the generations to follow. Generational wealth is created through the collaboration of people who are like-minded and who each accept a responsibility of creating and perpetuating wealth.

My son, Tyler, went on a mission trip to Africa in 2010 with a small group of college students. They flew into Dakar and then traveled 12 hours by van to a remote village outside of Senegal. The tribe they connected with had no written language and relies solely on storytelling. They stayed in the village with the tribe for four nights and participated in the evening storytelling. You see, for this tribe, the stories were not simply a means of entertainment but were essential to the tribe's survival. The tribe leader would teach about culture, family, and survival through the stories taught to them growing up. The kids would learn and participate in the work by day and listen to stories at night. Tyler saw firsthand the circle of life and generational planning in its purest form.

Our culture is much different. We tend to rely on our school system and reactive forms of communication to raise our children. There is little if no structure in place to proactively teach our children about money, financial literacy, and family culture.

This underscores the point that the catalyst for generational planning is not the wealth itself but rather the mindset which carries through the generations that can preserve the wealth and create an opportunity for future generations. The "spirit of the gift" from one generation to the next is what makes the generational plan cohesive. It is the common thread that pulls the family together generation after generation.

The idea of having a generational plan in place lives far beyond our lifetime. To carry forward the wisdom and wealth you have today to future generations of people who you may never meet is something much bigger than any one person.

If the idea of generational planning is energizing to you, then we can help guide you through the thought process of getting your plan in place. However, if this is something you don't care to think about, then it is best to understand your mindset now.

The Danger in Waiting to Figure Everything Out

I often hear the same comment from people who are grieving over the loss of their mother or father, "I am trying to figure everything out".

What a powerful comment: "I am trying to figure everything out." If you dissect this statement and consider what is being communicated with these words you quickly realize that "everything" encompasses a lot of things. You also realize that the word "trying" means that there was little if any guidance given from one generation to the next about what needs to be done.

To understand why there is such a disconnect between generations and how to help connect the dots, you must first understand the root of the problem. It is my belief that there are two primary reasons families fail to connect generationally:

1. Many people tend to believe that "everything" simply equates to financial related matters, but when it comes to "trying to figure everything out", "everything" is much more far-reaching than simply money and possessions. It literally includes "everything". What is "everything"? Everything includes anything relating to Family, Faith, Fitness,

Finance, Philanthropy, Education, and more.

2. For many families, there are up to four living generations: grandparents, parents, children, and their children's children. While some of these families have traditions that include vacations, special occasions, church attendance, and even closely held secret family recipes, very few have a shared family plan that reaches into future generations.

Imagine for a moment that the patriarch of your family gathered all generations together to outline a family legacy plan which included a meaningful discussion about what your family stands for, what values you share, what wealth strategies are in place, what to expect as one generation dies and a new one is born.

What if this were to happen? What if each family member and each generation had a responsibility to perpetuate the family plan? How powerful would this be for future generations?

Instead of each generation starting over and struggling with, "I am trying to figure everything out", you have an opportunity to equip your family for generations. You just need to think differently about what it means to lead a family and form a new mindset of what generational planning means.

This book was created as a tool to help you plan, organize, and design your generational plan. It is a guide designed to help lift the fog of the status quo and lead you on a path of discovery for a new way of thinking about your legacy.

Generational Planning Mindset

Our mindset or belief system is an accumulation of experiences in our life which have molded us into who we are and how we think. It is important to understand our mindset on different areas of our life because it influences and drives our behavior and attitude toward all things. In other words, our mindset is what determines the life we live.

So, what is your mindset? It really is your opinion about everything. Every day, you experience things that mold you into who you are, and when you have to make a decision, you draw from those past experiences, and the decision you make creates an outcome or a result in your life.

Generational Mindset Scorecard

You may need to ask yourself a few questions and begin thinking about where your mindset is on this idea of generational planning.

1. How often does your family discuss family culture and what does it means to be part of your family?

2. What life lessons do you want your kids to pass to your grandkids and their grandkids?

3. What actions do you want to see future generations take when it comes to philanthropy?

4. How do you view your current situation? Do you believe you have everything figured out or is your mind open to exploring possible improvements in your financial situation?

5. Do you view life insurance as an asset and something you want to own such as with real estate?

6. Do you have a strong opinion either way about whether to leave money to your family while you are alive or wait until death to distribute the assets?

7. What do you want future generations to know about managing and using money that will help them to both create and perpetuate wealth across all generations?

8. Do you tend to focus your attention on the rate of return on your money or are you more focused on building assets and the utilization of what you have?

Your answers to these questions highlight how you think about your family, your money, and your legacy. You may have strong opinions about a few of the questions and possibly some uncertainty with others. This is a starting point for creating a generational plan. To get where you are trying to go, you must first know where you are.

Generational Planning Mindset Scorecard

We have identified eight key areas to every generational plan. Depending on your mindset in each area and the circumstances surrounding your situation, this process can help you identify the opportunities you have for developing your generational plan.

Family Dynamics

It goes without saying that each family is different. Some families are very close while others seldom communicate. This experience has created your belief system or mindset about what family looks like. If your family is close and you have affection for them, it will likely lead a desire to do something beneficial for them. On the other hand, your mindset may very well lead you away from the idea of generational planning if your family is not close or not important to you.

While it is true that having kids and grandchildren who are close is often the motivating factor for generational planning, it is not the only purpose behind such a plan. Some people have a benevolent goal in their mind to perpetuate giving beyond their lifetime, which can also lead to the desire to have a generational plan.

Communication

What we have found is that families which educate and communicate with one another are much more likely to be successful with their generational planning than those who do not. A family that lives abundantly by sharing information and resources creates an environment of generosity and collaboration. They teach their kids how to think about money and educates them on how their wealth was created and managed.

Meanwhile, some families live in secrecy about their wealth and do not share their knowledge with one another. They tend not to educate their children on how their wealth was acquired, how it was managed, and how to think about money. This mindset leaves each generation starting over and figuring things out on their own.

It is important to note that just because something has always been a certain way does not mean that it has to continue to be that way. If there are situations or circumstances within your family that you would like to see changed, you may very well be the catalyst for changing the pattern. If you change your approach, you will likely see a different result.

Charity

In my book, *Common Sense*, I dedicated an entire chapter on charitable giving. I point out that...

For many of us, charitable giving is driven by an inherent desire to be a part of something bigger than ourselves. The act of giving makes us feel like we are making a difference in our community and impacting others in a positive way. A donation to a church, sponsoring a child's sports team, building a community center, or a forming a foundation allows us to leave a fingerprint on the next generation.

Charitable giving is a fundamental part of many families and is often included in estate plans where a church or other non-profit receives a one-time distribution from an estate.

When it comes to generational planning, the same principals we have discussed throughout this book apply. A generational mindset perpetuates the gifts and becomes part of each generation's DNA.

Though charitable giving is not a necessary function of a generational plan, what we find is that those who practice giving throughout their life tend to be more in tune with the idea of generational planning.

Open Mindedness

We all know people who go through life thinking they have everything figured out and who could not possibly learn anything new. In their mind, they have consumed all the information they need. They are people who don't let facts get in the way of their opinion and are unlikely candidates for generational planning.

An open mind and an interest in finding new ways to make your life and the lives of your family better are what is needed to formulate a generational plan. It's an attitude that if it is possible to enhance any part of life, then there is an eagerness to learn how to make it happen.

Life Insurance

One of the most effective tools for generational planning is life insurance. It has played a significant role in many of the wealthiest families' estate planning for generations. The ability to purchase hundreds of thousands or even millions of dollars of insurance to benefit the next generation is a guaranteed way to replace assets that were consumed within one generation and creates additional wealth for future generations.

An example of this can be explained in a scenario where a client, having $1,000,000, plans to leave $500,000 to each of his two daughters. The idea is that when they pass away, the girls receive this money and absorb it into their current situation. The money is consumed by the girls and in turn, leaves the grandchildren with nothing from the estate of their grandparents. This is a fairly typical example of what happens. It is the rags to rags in three generations we discussed earlier.

Now, what if we take this same scenario and add life insurance to enhance the outcome using the same $1,000,000?

If this $1,000,000 were used to purchase a $1,000,000 life insurance policy on the husband and a $1,000,000 life insurance policy on the wife, there could be an additional $1,000,000 added to the estate, now totaling $2,000,000. Money that was going to be distributed to the two girls has now been multiplied by 100% with no stock market risk.

Now, with proper planning, each of the girls receives her $500,000 as originally intended, while the other $1,000,000 can be used to prepare for another transfer of wealth to the next generation.

Now that the transfer from the first generation to the second generation has been made, the second generation then prepares for the third generation by utilizing the same concept.

This is the basic framework for how a family can create and perpetuate wealth for multiple generations utilizing life insurance. It allows for consumption in each generation with a strategy to replace the consumption with a life insurance death benefit that multiplies the transfer to the next generation.

Keep in mind that each family situation will differ in terms of dollar amounts and the exact wishes of the giver. This is simply a basic example of what is possible using life insurance.

Handing Your Assets

The mindset you have toward transferring your assets to the next generation is important in how you design your generational plan.

The entire concept of generational planning rests on the idea of each generation creating and perpetuating wealth. This idea alone is what separates traditional estate planning from generational planning. Estate planning simply distributes assets at your death to designated beneficiaries, at which point, the plan normally stops. In this scenario, the money is distributed and gone forever.

When it comes to generational planning, while it does include an estate-planning component, it typically does not distribute everything at once to beneficiaries but is designed to benefit multiple generations.

If you prefer to see your kids or favorite charity benefit from what assets you have while you are alive or prefer to simply distribute assets at your death, then a traditional estate plan may be something to consider. This would simply distribute your assets at your death, finalizing the plan. However, using the concepts we have discussed in this book, you can enhance the wealth transfer even if you have no interest in creating an actual generational plan.

Financial Legacy

Cash flow is the most important element to any financial plan. It is the need to have money available when you need it for the rest of your life. Knowing and understanding your chronological cash flow needs is critical for you to save and spend money with confidence.

How well you manage your cash flow will determine how effective you are with all areas of your planning, including generational planning. Managing cash flow goes way beyond budgeting; it is about discovering what money is flowing out of your control and creating strategies to have more money flowing back into your control. By having more money flow into your control, you have more money to retain and utilize for the rest of your life and for future generations.

Your Focus

One of the biggest areas of confusion for savers is a misunderstanding of what it means to grow assets. Often the mindset is to invest money in the stock market with a buy, hold, and hope approach. In other words, they operate under the assumption that the markets will go up. The difficulty in planning with this approach is that the outcome is unknown. The performance of an investment is unpredictable and can result in a loss as easily as it can a gain.

The goal with financial planning is to keep as much of your money in your control as possible. This enables you to coordinate your cash needs now or in the future with the resources you have in your control.

If your focus is solely on hypothetical rates of return, then trying to develop a generational plan may be a challenge because generational planning is not about rates of return. It is about having money flowing into your control and producing the most desirable outcome. The question to answer is whether you are investing or are you planning?

When you are able to articulate your mindset within these areas, you will have confidence in knowing what your ultimate goal is for your family and future generations. When you know and understand what is happening, you will know what to do.

Keeping the Money Together

As it was said by Cornelius Vanderbilt, "Keep the Money Together". Unlike many estate plans where money is divided up, distributed, and consumed, if you keep the money together, you leave your family with opportunity.

The most common use of money that is inherited has nothing to do with wealth creation and has everything to do with consumption. An inheritance is often used to make large purchases or to pay off debt. Wealth creation for future generations is not even a consideration in the majority of situations. A generational plan, on the other hand, allows future generations to access money for specific purposes that you deem to be worthy of a withdrawal.

Imagine for a moment that through your strategic planning your kids, grandkids, and future generations have access to money for school, starting a business, or their first home without ever having to go to a bank and without the obligation to pay it back until their death. The family could be free to use money from the estate, provided they have an insurance policy on their life to replace the money they consumed.

This is how you perpetuate wealth and it illustrates what you can do when you keep the money together. A move away from relying on banks and consumption is a move toward wealth creation. It is a mindset to be carried forward throughout your generational plan.

Family Constitution

When thinking generationally, it is important to clarify your wishes for how money is to be used and what values you want to pass along to future generations. Think of a Family Constitution as a letter you are writing that expresses your wishes and the spirit of how each generation is to handle the responsibility of the assets. The Family Constitution should explain the importance of "Keeping the money together" and why it is in their best interest to carry forward what you have established.

Your constitution should communicate the core values and wishes you have future generations to follow. This would include your thoughts and feelings about the family and provide guidance in the following areas:

Charity—You would outline your wishes for how money is to be given and guidelines for the type of charities to consider.

When charity is included in your planning, it can provide fulfillment for all of those involved. It brings a sense of gratitude and meaning to the generations.

Family—You would express your vision for how your family should work together in making the most of the current generation while building opportunity for future generations. You can describe what it means to be part of your family while listing the values you stand for.

This can bring a sense of unity to the family and also bring about a sense of appreciation for what the family stands for.

Wealth Creation—In an optimal generational plan, you would express the desire for family members to obtain the largest life insurance policy possible on each of their lives. If a family owned business is involved, you would also explain details of how the business is to be managed and additional wisdom you wish to pass on.

When the bar is set for each generation to create wealth for future generations, there is enthusiasm for what is possible and a sense of pride being a part of something bigger than themselves.

Utilization—Assets for your generational plan will be held in one or more trusts, depending on the size and complexity of your generational plan. You would explain how money could be accessed from the trusts and the responsibilities surrounding the utilization of the assets.

There is a TV series called *Last Man Standing*. Tim Allen plays Mike, the father of three daughters, Kristen, Mandy and Eve. In one particular episode, Mike and his wife, Vanessa, discuss plans to give each of their girls $20,000 for their weddings with a catch: They have to get married in their church. In the episode, Kristen announces plans to marry her boyfriend Ryan. Mike gives $20,000 to Kristen for her wedding, not knowing that the plans Ryan and Kristen have are to get married in the woods and use the money to pay off Ryan's student loans. As you can imagine, this does not sit well with Mike and Vanessa, and the episode plays out in dramatic form.

This is an example of how easily the spirit or meaning of a gift is distorted and consumed. Adding structure and limitations can help incentivize the desired behavior you have for future generations. The idea of encouraging higher education, the starting of a business, or some other action gives you control and a sense of confidence that the plan will foster the desired results.

Some have included a cash compensation for fulfilling certain activities such as receiving a college education, reading and preparing a book report for specific books, or fulfilling certain tasks or activities.

Management

Appointing a board of directors (BOD) for the management of the generational plan would help carry forward the constitution and the use of the assets of the trust. They would act on your behalf to carry out your wishes.

A BOD can help instill confidence in the plan design and a sense of formality that helps to keep the money together.

The details of such a plan are entirely up to you. You can expand or streamline this approach to accommodate your unique situation and satisfy your personal preferences.

Once you begin to think about the possibilities, you will likely feel a sense of hope and enthusiasm for what is possible. A generational plan can instill confidence for you and your family that, when done properly, can last for generations.

It is my hope that this book can be a catalyst to help expand your way of thinking about what is possible and bring about the opportunity for you and your family.

Myths and Mistakes Surrounding Generational Planning

After two decades of experience working in the area of estate and generational planning, I can say with confidence that there are many myths and consistent mistakes that are being made which prevent the creation and perpetuation of wealth from occurring.

Myths and Mistakes

Myth: It ties money up that I need to live on.
Mistake: People will dismiss the idea of generational planning with this limiting belief without learning more about how a plan actually works.
Reality: Many of the plan designs we use allow for access to cash throughout the giver's lifetime.

Myth: Estate Planning is only for the wealthy.
Mistake: People often forego any legal preparations with this line of reasoning without understanding the problems they are creating for themselves and their family.
Reality: Estate planning is beneficial for anyone who has children or liquid assets over $250,000.

Myth: I am too old or too young to be thinking about this.
Mistake: People will sometimes base their decision to do nothing on their personal limiting beliefs.
Reality: Generational planning is not about age. Anyone, young or old, who has the right mindset can be a catalyst for generational planning.

Myth: All I need are Transfer on Death (TOD) or Payable on Death (POD) on property titles or beneficiary designations on retirement accounts or insurance policies.
Mistake: People often believe that these designations are sufficient to pass their estate from themselves to someone else at their death. In many cases, this is an effort to avoid the expense of an attorney.
Reality: A TOD or POD designation only transfers the asset from one person to another, which is the primary problem with the status quo of wealth transfer. This mindset often leads to consumption.

Myth: My kids will know what to do.
Mistake: People will sometimes think because their children have a good education or job that it qualifies them to be a financial expert and know what to do.
Reality: A good education or successful career does not mean they know and understand financial or generational planning.

Myth: This is more of an opinion than it is a myth, but some people have a belief that their assets and wishes are private and are not anyone's business.

Mistake: While it is true they are your assets and are private, this mindset has proven, time after time, to cause problems within families.

Reality: I have had clients in my office on many occasions in tears over the fact their parents will not communicate anything with them. They are given no guidance and have to wait until their parent's death to learn what is going on.

Myth: Having a charity as a beneficiary disinherits my kids.

Mistake: Frequently, people neglect to leave money to their church or favorite charity believing any asset which goes to the charity is one less asset that goes to their kids.

Reality: The fact is that by utilizing life insurance and charitable trusts, often MORE money can be left to the children while giving money to the charity. Think about this: when working with charities, you have tax advantages which cut the IRS out as a beneficiary. This is more money to distribute to people and causes you care about.

Myth: This is another mindset which is more of an opinion than it is a myth but is worth, mentioning. There are some who gift assets to their children each year with the goal of helping their kids out while they are alive.

Mistake: This approach can drastically reduce the potential size of an estate and the transfer of assets from one generation to the next. While the idea behind this gift is to avoid estate taxes, it is not efficient and should only be considered after speaking with qualified professionals.

Reality: By using a specially designed life insurance policy, you have the ability to offer gifts to your children while simultaneously creating a tax-free death benefit. When you give money directly to your kids, you are potentially missing out on passing hundreds if not millions of dollars to your kids.

Myth: I already have a will and/or a trust.
Mistake: What we have found is that much of the legal work prepared simply distributes assets to their children and often does not resemble a generational plan.
Reality: Basic legal work simply passes money to the kids. This approach leaves the assets susceptible to consumption and leaves nothing for the next generation.

Myth: The life insurance I have is sufficient.
Mistake: Assuming the life insurance you have is sufficient to satisfy your plans is risky. The type, funding strategy, and duration of the policy all play a role in the viability or efficiency of the policy.
Reality: After careful review, we often find policies that were either not what the client thought they were or are simply a poorly designed contract. We have had clients bring us policies they thought were paid for when in fact, after review, were on pace to lapse within a few short years.

Anyone can come up with excuses for why this won't work or why it is not right for their family. However, your family is looking to you for guidance and leadership. How you think and what you do will impact your family for generations. The question is, what are you going to do about it?

There is really no limit to what can be done and this is why I took the time to write this book. We need to get this information into the hands of those who have or hope to have a generational mindset to give them the tools and information they need to fulfill their vision for their family.

Our process enables our clients to make decisions today, which will work toward satisfying their current and future financial needs while simultaneously maximizing the transfer of assets and ideas to the next generation. We work with clients to get them thinking beyond their situation and to think in terms of their legacy.

Create and Perpetuate Wealth For Generations...

A generational plan is to be considered an extension of a personal financial plan. Our number one priority is to make sure the client's needs are being met personally before we begin discussing the details of generational goals. We have a process we walk through as a team to clarify our client's goals and objectives. Everything we do and the recommendations we make will align with these goals and objectives.

Since everything is about having money available when you need it, our team works alongside of our clients to develop an effective cash flow strategy that is custom-tailored to meet the unique needs that each client has. This approach is designed to ensure money is available when they need it and outlines their short- and long-range goals.

We then incorporate the generational planning elements into the conversation and bring your personal and generational planning together. Our team of attorneys, advisors and counselors work with you to build out the framework for your generational plan. Together, we discuss strategies to bring what you envision for your family to life.

Once the framework for your generational plan is in place, we then incorporate your family members and other participants of your plan together. This allows for open discussion about the plan, what its purpose is, and reveals what the next steps are with your unique situation. Having a generational plan, communicating with your kids through a family constitution, and working with the same financial resources can help facilitate the goal of keeping the money together.

We invite you to reach out to us via email at: **yourmoney@sfgplan.com** or call our office at 636-296-5225 to see about starting your generational plan. You may be closer than you think.

Improve Your Mindset

Your mindset determines who you are, how you live and who you become. The Generational Planning Mindset Scorecard will help you track and improve the view you have that will lead to your future success when it comes to leaving a financial legacy for generations. Based on our experience, people with forward thinking mindsets will perform better as they work to create and perpetuate wealth for generations. I won't promise it will be easy, I promise it will be worth the effort.

To improve your generational planning mindset read this book and score yourself with the Generational Planning Scorecard. Share your results with us and we can help you develop a plan to improve your score.

Get started now at

www.GenerationalPlanningScorecard.com

About the Author - Brian Skrobonja

A native to St Louis, Missouri, Brian's father migrated from Croatia to Missouri a half a century ago and married his mother who was born and raised in St Louis. Growing up his mom and dad modeled the importance of family and having a strong work ethic. His father worked a full-time job while running a small business and his mother raised two children.

At a young age, Brian recognized the importance of working hard, living as an example and helping others. As the first generation born and raised in the United States, Brian has always been determined to lead a legacy for his family. He believes in challenging the status quo and thinking differently about what his role is as a father, husband and business owner.

In 1992, his family's tax accountant introduced Brian to the financial business and offered an opportunity to work for him. Brian took him up on the offer the following year and began working closely with a team of financial and tax professionals offering various products and services to clients.

After two years of being in the financial services business, he took his experience and opened his own financial planning business. Shortly after putting his name on the door Brian made a shift away from the financial industries approach of offering products and began focusing on his core belief of helping others and serving the unique planning needs of his clients.

Within a few short years, Brian built a network of professionals offering Tax, Mortgage, Insurance, Legal and Investment services becoming a comprehensive resource for his clients.

Brian has been interviewed on radio stations 97.1 with Dana Loesch and KMOX with Mark Reardon and Debbie Monterey. He authored a book titled Common Sense and he resides in the St Louis, Missouri area with his wife Kari and has three children Tyler, Malori, Hannah, a daughter in law Taylor, a grandson Waylon and a family dog Kooper.

For those of you wondering, Skrobonja is pronounced Skrō-bone-yŭ.

Create and Perpetuate Wealth For Generations…

You already know that at some point we are leaving this earth and our assets will pass on to our children. The challenging part of this reality is preventing a lifetime of wealth creation from flowing to your children to then be consumed.

That's where we come in. We help people just like you develop strategies to both create and perpetuate wealth that has the potential to last for multiple generations.

Step 1: To get started, it is helpful to learn and understand the mindset you have about money and the idea of generational planning. We all have a different perspective for how things are and how they should be. By first discovering your mindset, we can determine if you are good candidate for generational planning. Visit www.generationalplanningscorecard.com to complete your mindset exercise.

Step 2: For those who are a candidate for generational planning, we start with making sure you have a financial plan in place that's satisfying your current and future cash flow needs. Everything is about cash flow! So, we have to make sure your cash flow needs are being met before we can begin to plan generationally.

Step 3: We then begin to position assets to make sure you are taken care of while you are living and begin to arrange the transfer of assets to the next generation. We work with a team of financial advisors, attorneys, counselors and other professionals to put a cohesive plan in place.

Many people, when they think about their death, they think about the events that lead up to their death. There are very few who think about what will happen after their death and even fewer who think about their grandchildren, great grandchildren or generations that follow. There is seldom much thought about the ripple effects of our decisions for the future generations.

Now you can influence multiple generations by putting a plan in place that has the potential to create and perpetuate wealth for generations to come.

If you'd like our help, send an email to: **yourmoney@SFGPlan.com** to get started.

Disclosure:

Opinions voiced in this book are not intended to provide specific advice and should not be construed as recommendations for any individual. To determine which investments may be appropriate for you, consult with your financial, tax or legal professional.

Made in the USA
Lexington, KY
15 April 2017